A–Z of Intercultural Communication

Rudi Camerer & Judith Mader

A–Z of Intercultural Communication
by Rudi Camerer & Judith Mader

Academic Study Kit
81 Northwood Avenue
Brighton BN2 8RG
East Sussex
ENGLAND

www.academicstudykit.com

© Academic Study Kit 2016

The rights of Judith Mader and Rudi Camerer to be identified as the authors of this work have been asserted in accordance with the Copyright, Designs and Patents Act 1988.

All rights reserved. This book is in copyright, which normally means that no reproduction of any part may take place without the written permission of Academic Study Kit. The photocopying of certain parts of it by individual teachers for use within their classrooms, however, is permitted without such formality.

Pages which are copiable by the teacher without further permission are identified by PHOTOCOPIABLE © Academic Study Kit.

First published 2016

Edited by Judith Mader and Julie Pratten
Designed by Jovana Lukić
Cover design by Excell Design

ISBN 978-0-9524614-3-2

A CIP catalogue for this title is available at the British Library.

Acknowledgments:

Many thanks go to the trainers on our teacher-training courses and students on our courses who have used these activities and provided us with valuable feedback. Thanks also go to Julie Pratten for ideas and inspiration and to Helen Strong for the idea behind the Names activity.

Special thanks go to our children Julia, Charlotte, Philip, Gabriel, Naomi and Jessica who have all given us the benefit of their intercultural experiences in Europe, America, Africa, Australia and Asia and provided us with many new insights into intercultural communication.

References: Interkulturelle Kompetenz – Schlüsselkompetenz des 21. Jahrhunderts.
Thesenpapier der Bertelsmann Stiftung auf der Basis der interkulturellen
Kompetenzmodelle von Dr. Darla Deardorff. Gütersloh 2006 (authors' translation).

Contents

Introduction	4-5
Error Analysis	6
How to use the Activities	7
Contents map	8
Trainer's notes and Task sheets	10-67

INTRODUCTION

A-Z of Intercultural Communication is a collection of stimulating activities for intercultural communication practice for intermediate to advanced learners of English. The activities have been tried and tested around the world with many different groups of learners, university students, and learners in companies and on training courses in intercultural communication. They are particularly suitable for university students and pre-experience learners.

Everyone involved in international business as well as academic life needs intercultural communication skills if they are going to be successful and function effectively in their studies and their careers. The competences they need include knowledge, attitudes and communicative abilities. All of these areas are addressed in this material.

The knowledge required for successful intercultural communication is of two types. Firstly knowing that differences exist between cultures is important. This may not always be clear to those who have little international or intercultural experience. In general, learners know that there are different types of food and dress and that weather is different in different countries, but may well not be aware of differences between cultures, for instance in attitudes to time, hierarchy, gender, education, politeness and other things.

The term culture does not necessarily mean a national culture, although national differences are most often the focus when describing cultural differences. Culture can also be corporate, religious or regional within a country. In addition it should not always be assumed that any specific culture is always the reason for differences or difficulties which arise in communication; these may well be caused by individual differences and have little or nothing to do with nationality, ethnicity, religion or culture.

When dealing with other people from a different national or cultural background or travelling to another country, particularly for business or educational reasons, it is important to have a second type of knowledge, that of specific features of the country and the context. This can involve facts such as the name of the capital of the country, the main language(s) spoken and the political system. Information about the specific context, the educational institution or the company or sector will also be invaluable so as not to appear uninterested, ill-informed or ignorant. Also useful are so-called dos and don'ts connected with the context, such as how to address people, table manners and taboo topics, again to name but a few.

It is also important to have an appropriate attitude towards intercultural communication and to be as open-minded, tolerant and flexible as possible. The activities in A-Z of Intercultural Communication, however, do not make any attempt to analyse or change learners' attitudes or personality for two reasons. Firstly, when dealing with adults, attitudes and personalities are not easy to change (if this is at all possible!) and secondly, everyone involved with intercultural communication will at some point reach the limits of what they are able to accept. For these two reasons, the focus in the activities here is on the raising of awareness of differences and on practical communicative skills, both of which can be used in a range of different contexts.

Intercultural competence is an ideal combination of knowledge and personality but also, and perhaps most importantly, involves communicative skills. This means being able to deal with situations and resolve difficulties using language. The language used in intercultural communication will probably in most cases be English, whether in the UK or another English-speaking country or in fact anywhere in the world. For this reason, language and communication skills are the focus of many of the activities.

The main aspects we deal with in our courses in intercultural communication cover the following areas: intercultural theory and its relevance to communication, corporate and educational culture and the specific issues involved in these, mediation, negotiation and meta-communication, politeness conventions in different contexts and the use of English as a lingua franca.

We deal with these in various ways and often in the context of critical incidents. These are incidents in which aspects of culture cause misunderstanding, irritation or confusion for those involved. Although the reasons for critical incidents are interesting and important, our focus is on how the difficulties arising can be resolved and how similar incidents may be avoided in future. We make a lot of use of our learners' own experiences and the difficulties they may have encountered in intercultural communication as well as drawing on our own wide experience in the field.

Any course can naturally only achieve a limited amount of success and the extent of individual knowledge, attitudes, communicative skills and experience will always play an essential part in the success or failure of real intercultural communication outside the protected environment of a training programme.

There are four things which need to be remembered:

- You never meet a culture, but always meet individuals.
- You cannot not communicate.
- Always try to be non-judgemental.
- Always be as well-prepared as possible!

There are many more things which could be added, but these probably encapsulate the essence of our view on successful intercultural communication which lies behind the activities.

We hope you enjoy using A-Z of Intercultural Communication.

Judith Mader & Rudi Camerer

"Intercultural Competence means possessing the necessary attitudes and reflective and behavioural skills and using these to behave effectively and appropriately in intercultural situations."

Darla Deardorff

Error-analysis sheet

Name: _____ **Date:** _____

Good use of language

....
....
....
....
....

Errors

....
....
....
....
....
....
....

Look at the errors above. How could you correct them?

Things to work on

....
....
....
....
....

HOW TO USE THE ACTIVITIES

A-Z of Intercultural Communication is a collection of stimulating activities designed to raise awareness of intercultural issues and provide ways of dealing with these interactively.

Who are the activities for?
The activities are designed for intermediate to advanced learners of English. The focus is not on correctness of language but its appropriacy in intercultural situations. The activities work very well with multi-cultural and multi-national groups as well as groups with different language levels. Although the term student has been used throughout, they are also suitable for other types of learners.

How can the activities be used?
The tasks can be used in any order depending on your needs; for self-study, one-to-one teaching and in groups. The activities can be used to lead into a particular topic or as revision after a topic has been dealt with. They can also be used as warm-up activities in general English courses to stimulate discussion and encourage communication between learners.

How are the activities structured?
The title of the activity generally relates to a specific topic dealt with in courses in intercultural communication. Each activity consists of trainer's notes and a task sheet for learners, usually one page. In some cases, there are two task sheets on one page. These may include slightly different tasks for each learner.

The trainer's notes include information on the focus of the task, how long the task will take and the type of activity (pair work, group work etc.). Symbols are used for this. The duration will depend on the size and composition of the group and whether and how extensively the follow-up activities are used. The task sheets include follow-up activities.

If you want more background information on intercultural theory and intercultural competence and on how to set up courses and teach intercultural communication, we recommend you look at *Intercultural Competence in Business English* published by Cornelsen, Berlin in 2012.

We hope you enjoy using these activities and would love to hear your ideas for further A-Z activity books.

ACTIVITY TYPES

 Individual work   Presentations

 Pair work   Problem-solving exercises

 Group work   Discussions

For links go to www.academicstudykit.com

CONTENTS MAP

	activity	focus	type	duration	page
A	Awareness	stereotypes and perceptions		20	10
B	Body language	body language		15	12
C	Critical incidents	describing and explaining intercultural difficulties		15	14
D	Differences and similarities	cultural differences and similarities		20	16
E	Emails	effective email writing in different intercultural settings		40	18
F	Foods	food		20	20
G	Getting to know people	politeness conventions		20	22
H	Hi	hedging and fielding difficult questions in intercultural settings		20	24
I	Intercultural communication	introduction to culture		30	26
J	Judgement	judgemental statements, stereotypes		10	28
K	Knowledge	facts about countries		15	30
L	Low context	cultural theory		20	32
M	Models	describing cultures		20	34

CONTENTS MAP

	activity	focus	type		duration	page
N	Names	stereotypes and preconceptions	👤	🖥️	20	36
O	Own critical incidents	critical incidents	👥 👥		20	38
P	Politeness	politeness	👥 👥		20	40
Q	Quotations	definitions of culture	👥 👥		20	42
R	Responses	polite discourse	👥 👥		10	44
S	Strange and normal	cultural assumptions	👥 👥		20	46
T	Time	cultural assumptions	💥	💿	30	48
U	Universals	cultural universals	👤	💿	15	50
V	Very bad behaviour	cultural assumptions	💥	💿	15	52
W	Where would(n't) you?	polite behaviour	👤	💿	20	54
X	X-word	intercultural theory	👤		20	56
Y	You think…	appropriate reactions	👥 👥		20	58
Z	QuiZZZ	facts about Britain	👤 👥		15	60

AWARENESS

Focus: stereotypes and preconceptions

Duration: 20 minutes

Activity type:

Trainer's notes

1. Photocopy the task sheet for each student. In addition, give each student a small piece of paper.
2. Lead-in: Discuss what culture can mean - national, regional, family, company, professional, religious or another. In a multinational group, each student can choose their national culture, in a group where several students are from one country or area, students should choose a different culture.
3. Explain to students that they should think about which culture/s they belong to. Once they have decided and written this on the piece of paper, they should find someone with (a) different answer/s.
4. Hand out the tasks.
5. Follow the instructions for the task.
6. Students answer the questions individually for themselves and then for their partners.
7. In pairs they ask each other the questions and compare the answers they gave for their partners.

Follow-up

Discuss differences in the answers and what they are based on – stereotypes, pre-conceptions, mistakes, assumptions?

AWARENESS

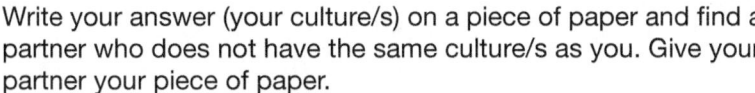

Think about:
How far do you represent your culture/s?
What culture/s do you belong to?

Write your answer (your culture/s) on a piece of paper and find a partner who does not have the same culture/s as you. Give your partner your piece of paper.

Now, working on your own, give your personal answers to these questions.

1. What is your favourite food?

2. What do you usually wear?

3. How do you greet people?

4. Where do you usually have lunch?

5. What time do you start work?

6. What sort of weather do you like best?

7. How many languages do you speak?

Remember:
Culture can be national, regional, family, company, professional, religious or another. In fact: every individual belongs to several cultures, the particular mix of cultures stands for much of what is considered that person's individuality!

How far do you think your answers are representative of the culture/s you gave above?

Now answer the questions for your partner's culture/s. Base your answers on what you know of the culture and not the person.

How far do your partner's personal answers correspond to your ideas?

BODY LANGUAGE

Focus: body language

Duration: 15 minutes

Activity type:

Trainer's notes

1. Photocopy the task sheet for each pair of students and cut in half.
2. Tell students to decide individually about each example of body language and then discuss them with their partner.
3. Those who finish quickly can then think of more examples of polite / rude body language?

Follow-up

- Discuss the difference between body language and gestures and elicit examples of each and what they mean in different cultures.
- Think of more examples of unacceptable body language and gestures.

KEY - BODY LANGUAGE

The following are considered rude in many cultures:

Blowing your nose
Eating with your mouth open
Sitting with your legs crossed
Sitting with your legs apart
Staring at the person you are talking to
Pointing at the person you are talking to

The following may be acceptable in some cultures:

Holding up one finger to make a point
Looking at the floor when someone is talking to you
Folding your arms in front of your chest
Looking away when someone is talking to you

The following may depend on the situation and people involved:

Taking off a piece of clothing (e.g. shoes, tie, T-shirt)
Yawning
Sniffing
Picking your teeth
Looking at the ceiling when someone is talking to you
Pointing at someone you are talking about
Adjusting a piece of clothing (e.g. bra, tie, belt)
Sighing

BODY LANGUAGE

Task sheet A

Are the following examples of body language
(when other people are there)

a) polite

b) fully acceptable

c) sometimes acceptable

d) generally inacceptable

e) rude or very rude

in your culture?

Confidential! Do not show this copy to your partner!

Answer the questions yourself first and then discuss your answers
with a partner and the whole group.

Blowing your nose	Yawning
Eating with your mouth open	Sniffing
Holding up one finger to make a point	Picking your teeth
Looking at the floor when someone is talking to you	Folding your arms in front of your chest
Pointing at the person you are talking to	Looking at the ceiling when someone is talking to you
Sitting with your legs crossed	Pointing at someone you are talking about
Looking away when someone is talking to you	Sitting with your legs apart
Taking off a piece of clothing (e.g. shoes, tie, T-shirt)	Staring at the person you are talking to
Pointing finger	Adjusting a piece of clothing (e.g. bra, tie, belt)
	Sighing

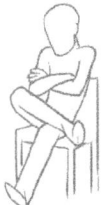

CRITICAL INCIDENTS

Focus: describing and explaining intercultural difficulties

Duration: 15 minutes

Activity type: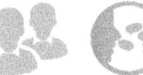

Trainer's notes

1. Photocopy task sheet A and B and give a task sheet to each pair
2. Tell students to follow the instructions and describe the incident to their partner. Do not let them read out the incident. They should explain it in their own words as far as possible.
3. Ask students to discuss the incidents one by one and answer the questions.
4. Collect their answers and discuss the best solutions in the whole group.

Follow-up

Discuss which style of teaching students prefer and how they think it is best to learn a foreign language.

CRITICAL INCIDENTS

Task sheet A

A critical incident
- happens unexpectedly
- produces negative reactions or feelings
- makes an impression
- needs a solution

Tell your partner what happens in this incident, ask and answer questions and discuss possible solutions. Listen to your partner's incident and do the same. Then discuss the differences.

 **Confidential! Do not show this text to your partner!**

> Helena from Germany was doing her PhD in Japanese studies and was in Japan to do some research. The university asked her to teach some advanced German classes. In the first class, she introduced herself in German with "Hi, my name's Helena". She was surprised when the students replied, "Good morning Professor". Then she asked the students to tell her about themselves. No-one came forward so she asked each one individually. Each student stood up, said their name and sat down. She asked some questions which they answered in good German. Then she asked them to discuss environmental protection in small groups and give their opinions on questions which she wrote on the board. Nothing happened. Eventually she gave them a dictation and then handed out a text which she had prepared for the discussion. She wrote vocabulary on the board which the students copied down. Their German was clearly at an advanced level. At the end of the class they left without a word.

*for TASK SHEET B go to page 62

DIFFERENCES AND SIMILARITIES

Focus: cultural differences and similarities

Duration: 20 minutes

Activity type:

Trainer's notes

1. Photocopy the task for each student.
2. Lead-in: Write the names of countries students are from on the board. If all the students are from one country, elicit countries they have been to or feel they know well and write these on the board. In this case, ask each person to choose one country.
3. Hand out the tasks.
4. Ask students individually to make their own questionnaire and to interview a partner. They should then report on the differences between their cultures.
5. Working in pairs, they should then find as many similarities between their cultures as possible. These can be of any sort, connected with attitudes, geography, political system, size etc.

Follow-up

- Brainstorm stereotypes about these countries (see also S for Stereotypes) and discuss these.
- Students find out (Internet research) if the stereotypes are confirmed by facts.
- Discuss the usefulness or otherwise of stereotypes.
- In groups, students make a poster about a particular country (their own or one they are interested in).
- Students prepare a short presentation on a particular country (their own or one they are interested in).

LINKS
Country profiles

DIFFERENCES AND SIMILARITIES

Here are some common differences between cultures:

- Extrovert / introvert
- Attitude to work
- Rules and flexibility
- Attitude to time
- Attitude to power
- Formal / informal
- Attitude to space
- National pride

Can you think of any more?

What questions would you ask to find out about these?

Write them down.

Remember:
In intercultural communication, you can focus on differences but also on similarities, i.e. things you have in common, which often makes communication easier.

Find someone from another culture or country to your own and ask them the questions.

Note the differences between your cultures and present the differences you find to the class.

Now try and find as many similarities between your countries as you can.

E-MAILS

Focus: effective email writing in different intercultural settings

Duration: 40 minutes

Activity type:

Trainer's notes

1. Photocopy the task for each student.
2. Lead-in: Ask students for examples of emails they find difficult to write and why.
3. Hand out the tasks.
4. Follow the instructions for the task.
5. Hang the emails up in the classroom and let students walk around, compare them and suggest improvements.

Follow-up

Write other difficult emails, e.g.

- Making a request, refusing the request and making a repeat request.
- Changing an arranged appointment, asking why the appointment wasn't kept and apologising for not turning up
- Refusing an invitation to a university event
- Asking why a professor was not in the office at a time arranged for an appointment
- Requesting an extension of a deadline for a term paper
- Giving feedback on another student's presentation which was not very good
- Apologising for absence at an important class
- Objecting to a grade a teacher has given and asking for an explanation

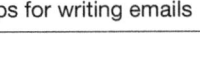
Tips for writing emails

E-MAILS

Look at this email from a student asking a professor for an extension of a term paper deadline.

```
From: coolguy.Rosh@hotmail.com
To: a.illman@uni-hull.edu
Re.: Hi!

Hello there miss professor,
I have some problem with your dear line for my pepper.
Can I give it to you one week later. You see, I have a very
important football training this week and have no time to
finish it. I think this is okay.

See you later

Your student
Roshan Hale
```

Some aspects of emails are mentioned below. Decide if they are good, acceptable or need improving in the email above. Then discuss how the email could be improved with a partner.

	Good?	Acceptable?	Needs improving?
Email address			
Subject of email			
Salutation – how you begin a letter/an email			
Close – how you end a letter or an email			
Main message			
Politeness			
Spelling			

Write an improved version of this email in a group. Decide which email is best.

*refer to page 63 for Tips about writing emails

FOOD

Focus: food

Duration: 20 minutes

Activity type:

Trainer's notes

1. Photocopy the task for each student.
2. Make sure students know all the words which occur in the task and which may come up in the session. Elicit or pre-teach some or all if necessary. The following categories may be useful: Food / ingredients / dishes / adjectives to describe food (positive/negative).
3. Hand out the tasks.
4. Follow the instructions for the task.

Follow-up

- Take students on an excursion to a market, food hall or delicatessen to find out more about local food.
- Students present a particular food or dish from your country.
- Students write a recipe for a dish from their country.
- Students bring some food from their country for the others to try.

LINKS

Marmite

Opinions about food

Unusual delicacies

Weird food combinations

FOOD

Food is often a difficult issue in general and perhaps especially in intercultural encounters. Answer the following questions and then interview a partner:

What food do you never eat? Why not?
What is the most unusual food you have ever eaten?
What is an unusual food or dish in your country?

Collect a list of possible reasons for not eating certain food. The following may help:

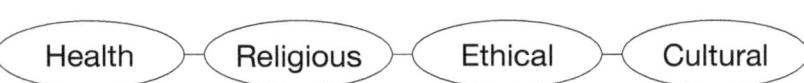

Health — Religious — Ethical — Cultural

Can you think of examples of food for each of them?
How do you feel about the following food?
Under what circumstances would you eat it?

MENU
Dog
Cat
Raw meat
Birds
Meat on the bone
Shellfish (prawns etc.)
Pork
Insects
Flowers
Intestines
Brain

Remember
Food is often a very sensitive topic, so it is important to be careful about how you refuse food in different cultures.

*for USEFUL LANGUAGE go to page 64

GETTING TO KNOW PEOPLE

Focus: politeness conventions

Duration: 20 minutes

Activity type:

Trainer's notes

1. Photocopy the task and cut along the dotted lines. Give one slip to each student.
2. Students interview each other and collect answers.
3. Students visualise the results of their survey and present these to the class.

Follow-up

- Discuss the differences in the answers.
- Discuss how people react when someone does one of these things at a first meeting.
- Ask for further ideas of what is appropriate and inappropriate at first meetings.

GETTING TO KNOW PEOPLE

Ask some other students what they do and say when they meet someone for the first time. Write down all the answers you get. Make a list or a mind map and present your results to the class.

When you meet people for the first time...

1. When you meet people for the first time, how do you greet them?

2. When you meet people for the first time, who speaks first?

3. When you meet people for the first time, what name do you give (your first name, your surname, all your names, your nickname...?).

4. When you meet people for the first time, do you smile or look serious?

5. When you meet people for the first time, do you shake hands or kiss?

6. When you meet people for the first time, do you compliment them on their clothes or hair?

7. When you meet people for the first time, do you invite them somewhere (to your house, a café ...)?

8. When you meet people for the first time, what do you tell them about yourself?

9. When you meet people for the first time, what do you ask them?

HI

Focus:	hedging and fielding difficult questions in intercultural settings
Duration:	20 minutes
Activity type:	

Trainer's notes

1. Photocopy the task for each student.
2. Lead-in: Read the story to students or tell it as if it happened to you.
3. Ask students to read the story and clarify any questions.
4. Ask students for their comments.
5. Students work individually and put the questions into two groups – appropriate and inappropriate questions for a first encounter.
6. Then ask them to compare their results with another student and come to a consensus on the appropriacy / inappropriacy of the questions.
7. This can be continued until a consensus is reached in the whole group or the different pairs / groups can be asked to present their results.

Follow-up

- Students change the questions to make them appropriate.
- Students decide what they would answer if asked these questions.
- Students think of strategies to use when asked questions they do not want to answer.
- Some suggestions are
- change the subject
- lie
- ask a different question
- say: - "I'm afraid I'd rather not say."
  - "That's an interesting question. I don't really know how to answer it."
  - "I'd rather not answer that question if you don't mind."

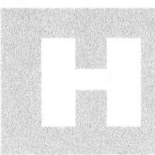

HI

Read this story:

> I have often been surprised by questions people ask me or things they tell me when they hardly know me. A mother I met at my daughter's kindergarten told me that her husband had been married before to someone who looked like me and another mother asked me how I had persuaded my husband to have three children! These were more or less the first things they said to me after "Hello, I'm …"
> In other contexts, I have been asked who I voted for in the last election. I have travelled a lot so some of the people who asked these things were from cultures quite different from European cultures, but I was still surprised.

Have you ever been in a situation like this?

What questions can you ask someone you have just met? Sort these questions into 2 groups – suitable for a first meeting and inappropriate for a first meeting. Think about your reasons for this and then discuss them with a partner.

- How much do you weigh?
- Are you religious?
- Are you married?
- How many children have you got?
- Are you gay?
- Are you a virgin?
- Where did you buy your shoes?
- What size do you take in trousers?
- Do you belong to a political party?
- What did you vote in the last election?
- Where do you live?
- Do you own your home?
- Have you got a driving licence?
- How big is your house?
- Are you a vegetarian?

How would you answer?
What could you say if you didn't want to answer the question?

INTERCULTURAL COMMUNICATION

Focus: introduction to culture

Duration: 30 minutes

Activity type:

Trainer's notes

1. Photocopy one copy of the task for each student.
2. Lead-in: before handing out the sheet, write Culture on the board and ask the first questions.
3. Elicit the factors defining culture and write them (and any others suggested) on the board.
4. Hand out the worksheet and clarify any questions.
5. Ask students for their comments.
6. Students work individually and decide on their answers to the questions and then compare them in groups.

Follow-up

- Discuss the following questions:
  - What aspects of behaviour in your culture / country would you describe as "normal" to a visitor?
  - What would you say is "typical" for your culture? In groups (from the same culture if possible) decide on something you can describe as typical for your country or culture and decide how you would describe it and its significance to a visitor.

Tips for classroom debates

- Conduct a debate.
  It is often said that globalisation means that cultures become more and more alike. Do you agree? Give reasons for and against this position.

INTERCULTURAL COMMUNICATION

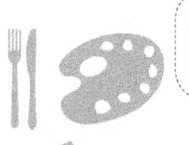

How would you define the word culture?

Here are some factors which are sometimes said to define cultures:

- agriculture and food
- art and literature
- attitudes to money and business
- buildings and architecture
- educational institutions
- geographical position and climate
- history
- language
- political system
- religious beliefs

Remember
Culture has many meanings and can be interpreted in many different ways.

Which of these things would you do / perhaps do / never do? Why (not)? Are your reasons personal or cultural?

Accept a marriage partner your parents choose for you.

Arrive at an important appointment (e.g. a job interview) 20 minutes late.

Eat an animal which is regarded as a pet.

Interrupt an important business partner or superior when they are talking.

Kiss someone when meeting them for the first time.

Start eating without saying anything.

Use someone's first name without explicitly being allowed to.

Think of some more examples!

JUDGEMENT

Focus: judgemental statements, stereotypes

Duration: 10 minutes

Activity type:

Trainer's notes

1. Photocopy the task for each student.
2. Students do the task and compare answers.
3. Discuss what is wrong with the judgemental statements.

Follow-up

Change the judgemental statements to make them more acceptable.

KEY - JUDGEMENT

1. Cars made in my country are the best in the world. Their design is perfect. __J__
2. During my last holiday in Britain I ate some wonderful food. __R__
3. Everyone knows that English food is bad. __J__
4. French people are unpunctual. They are always late for everything. __J__
5. Germans drink a lot of beer and are very rude. __J__
6. I would say that if Italians were totally disorganised, they would not be able to run a country. __R__
7. Just because something is different doesn't mean it is bad. __R__
8. Politeness is expressed in different ways in different cultures and languages. __R__
9. The Italians are completely disorganised and can't run any business properly. __J__
10. We all have different concepts of time and communicate differently about it. __R__
11. We must be careful about stereotypes. __R__
12. Mediterranean people are very emotional. __J__

JUDGEMENT

Which of these statements are judgemental? Mark them with a J. Which could you use to reply to a judgemental statement? Mark them with an R.

1. Cars made in my country are the best in the world. Their design is perfect. ___

2. During my last holiday in Britain I ate some wonderful food. ___

3. Everyone knows that English food is bad. ___

4. French people are unpunctual. They are always late for everything. ___

5. Germans drink a lot of beer and are very rude. ___

6. I would say that if Italians were totally disorganised, they would not be able to run a country. ___

7. Just because something is different doesn't mean it is bad. ___

8. Politeness is expressed in different ways in different cultures and languages. ___

9. The Italians are completely disorganised and can't run any business properly. ___

10. We all have different concepts of time and communicate differently about it. ___

11 We must be careful about stereotypes. ___

12. Mediterranean people are very emotional. ___

Remember
In intercultural communication it is important not to be judgemental about cultural differences, so as not to offend or anger the people you are talking to.

KNOWLEDGE

Focus: facts about countries

Duration: 15 minutes

Activity type:

Trainer's notes

1. Photocopy the task sheet for two students and cut into 2.
2. Student A works with student B.
3. Each student chooses a different country. It can be their own country or any country they know well.
4. Students ask each other the questions.

Follow-up

Discuss whether all the information is important and if there is any more information you need to know before visiting a country or getting to know someone from the country.

Talk about a country you have visited or plan to visit. What knowledge of that country did/do you have before your trip?

LINKS
Country profiles
World factbook

KNOWLEDGE

Student A

Ask your partner the following questions about a country or culture they know. Then answer the questions your partner asks you. Use your own experience to give the answers. If you don't know the information where can you find out?

KNOWLEDGE
1. How do people greet members of their family?
2. Who is the most popular politician?
3. Which sport do people watch most?
4. Which words of the language should foreigners learn?
5. What is a typical national dish?
6. What is one thing you should never do?
7. Have things changed a lot in the last 10 years?
8. What is the most important piece of news at the moment?

Student B

Ask your partner the following questions about a country or culture they know. Then answer the questions your partner asks you. Use your own experience to give the answers. If you don't know the information where can you find out?

KNOWLEDGE
1. How do people greet friends?
2. Who is the most popular film star?
3. Which sport do people play most?
4. Which words of the language should foreigners learn?
5. What is a typical national drink?
6. What is one thing you should always do?
7. Have things changed a lot in the last 20 years?
8. What is the most important piece of news at the moment?

LOW CONTEXT

Focus: cultural theory

Duration: 20 minutes

Activity type:

Trainer's notes

1. Photocopy the task for each student.
2. Lead-in: Ask students if they know anything about cultural theory and can name any cultural theorists. Write the terms high context, low context, proxemics, monochronic and polychronic on the board and ask students if they can imagine what these mean in terms of culture. If necessary, pre-teach any of the words in the text which may be unfamiliar.
3. Photocopy one copy of worksheet for each student.
4. Ask students to read the text. Discuss the information in the text.
5. Ask students to complete the table and check the answers.
6. Continue with the next exercise.

Follow-up

Reformulate the sentences as examples from the opposite context. Find out about the dimensions of proxemics and monochronic and polychronic time, also identified by Edward Hall.

KEY - LOW CONTEXT

High context communication   Low context communication
a c g i   b d e f h j

Examples of low and high context communication

a) high   c) low   e) low   g) high
b) low   d) low   f) high   h) low

LOW CONTEXT

The cultural dimensions of low and high context were identified by the US American cultural anthropologist Edward Hall (1914 –2009) in his 1976 book *Beyond Culture*. Edward Hall was one of the earliest influential and cross-cultural researchers. He identified and defined the dimensions of proxemics, monochronic and polychronic time, and low and high context communication to explain how people in different cultures behave and react.

High and low context refer to the way cultures use context in communication. Speaking style is connected to how much a culture consists of groups with similar experiences and expectations which can be referred to without being explicitly mentioned. The terms high and low context are relative. In higher-context cultures, many things are left unsaid as they need no explanation but are obvious from the context. This means that words and word choice are important in high-context communication. A message, even a complex one, can be conveyed in a small number of words. However to those unfamiliar with the context, what is meant may be hard to understand. In a lower-context culture, communication is much more explicit and individual words become less important as a number of words can be used to explain the context and the message. Questions can be asked and information repeated.

Remember
Cultural dimensions are only a guideline to cultures. They are useful as a general orientation rather than absolute and reliable ways of describing "national cultures".

Put the following features of communication into the two categories below:

(High context communication)   (Low context communication)

a) details
b) explicit descriptions
c) few words
d) explanations
e) implicit references
f) inferences
g) many words
h) mutual experiences
i) repetitions
j) unmentioned events

Decide which of these are examples of low and which of high context communication.

a) You must be tired.
b) Would you like to go to bed now?
c) The meeting will start at 10:10 pm. sharp so be on time.
d) In our meetings, the chairperson usually sits at the end of the table.
e) I am going to make you something to eat now.
f) Have you eaten?
g) You know what it is like here.
h) I will explain how you use this machine. There is also an instruction booklet.

MODELS

Focus: describing cultures

Duration: 20 minutes

Activity type:

Trainer's notes

1. Photocopy the task for each student.
2. Lead-in: Discuss what culture is – different layers, some things hidden, may be dangerous, always moving, dynamic, made up of several things, different aspects useful in different situations, something you have with you. Make clear that you are talking about the term culture and not a particular culture.
3. Ask students if they can think of an object which describes culture.
4. Give students the worksheet and ask them to explain how the objects describe culture.
5. Students answer the questions individually and then discuss their answers with others.

Follow-up

In groups, students find another object which could be used to describe culture and make a poster explaining this.

MODELS

TASK

The following have all been used to describe culture.

Think of your own answers to these questions and then discuss them with other students.

1 In which ways do these things describe a culture?
___

2 Which one do you find the most helpful?
___

3 Do you think they can be used to describe culture in general or might one be more useful for a particular culture?
___

4 Which other models can you think of which might be useful for describing a culture?
___

NAMES

Focus: stereotypes and preconceptions

Duration: 20 minutes

Activity type:

Trainer's notes

1. Photocopy the task for each student.
2. Lead-in: Write your own name on the board as an example and draw a mind map. Ask students what could be included in the mind map. Elicit, as far as possible, meaning, origin, famous people with the same name…
3. Follow the instructions on the worksheet.
4. Mind maps can be hung up in the classroom. Students can walk around and ask questions about the mind maps.
5. To show students what the presentations* involve, demonstrate by giving a short presentation on your own name.
6. Presentations can be prepared and given individually or in pairs. Encourage the others in the class to ask questions.

Follow-up

- Give some background to names in different cultures.
- Design a form taking into account different name conventions in different cultures.
- Students write a short text about their name or naming conventions in their culture.

LINKS

Some background to names

Personal names

What's behind a name

NAMES

Write your name clearly on a piece of paper. Then make a mind map around it.

Here are some questions which may help. These are just ideas. You may think of more.

1. How many names do you have?
2. What is the usual order for names in your country / culture?
3. Is your surname common?
4. Are your first names typical for boys / girls?
5. Are your given names common?
6. Does your name mean anything?
7. Are there famous people with the same name as you?
8. Is there any religious significance to your name?
9. Who chose your given name? Why?
10. Is your name easy to pronounce?
11. Is there a short form?
12. Should you have a different name for foreigners if yours is hard to pronounce?

Remember
Your name may be difficult for others to pronounce and / or remember so try and make it easy for others in some way (spelling it, simplifying it, shortening it).

Now find a partner and explain your name to him / her. Ask each other questions. You may use the questions above or think of your own.

Prepare a short presentation on your name. Divide the presentation into sections, one for each part of your name. The following phrases may help you.

Now I am going to give you some information about...

In the first part I will...

Then I will talk about...

Finally I will explain...

OWN CRITICAL INCIDENTS

Focus:	critical incidents
Duration:	20 minutes
Activity type:	

Trainer's notes

1. Photocopy the task for each student.
2. Lead-in: Ask students (individually or in groups) what a critical incident is and what you need to know in order to explain or understand it. Elicit one or two examples of critical incidents from students and ask questions about details (or let other students ask the questions).
3. Photocopy the task sheet and cut it in half for each pair.
4. Ask students to think about a critical incident they have experienced and answer the questions as far as they can.

Follow-up

- Ask students if it is necessary to know the answers to all the questions and if there are other questions they would ask about a critical incident.
- Write a description of a critical incident you have experienced or heard about without judging or explaining it.
- Exchange descriptions and write a possible explanation for the critical incident.

OWN CRITICAL INCIDENTS

Think of a critical incident you have experienced. Answer these questions. Then describe it to your partner.

CRITICAL INCIDENTS

- Where and when did it happen?
- Who were the people involved?
- What information do you have about them (age, gender, relationship, nationality, profession etc?)
- What part did you play?
- What happened?
- How did the people feel?
- What happened then?
- What were the reasons?
- Can you suggest a solution?

Remember
A critical incident is an occurrence which causes misunderstanding, possibly leading to further consequences.

Think of a critical incident you have experienced. Answer these questions. Then describe it to your partner.

CRITICAL INCIDENTS

- Where and when did it happen?
- Who were the people involved?
- What information do you have about them (age, gender, relationship, nationality, profession etc?)
- What part did you play?
- What happened?
- How did the people feel?
- What happened then?
- What were the reasons?
- Can you suggest a solution?

Remember
A critical incident is an occurrence which causes misunderstanding, possibly leading to further consequences.

POLITENESS

Focus: politeness

Duration: 20 minutes

Activity type:

Trainer's notes

1. Photocopy the task for each student.
2. Lead-in: Ask the group to define politeness.
3. Ask students (individually or in groups) for examples of polite and rude behaviour in their own cultures.
4. Photocopy the task sheet for each student or group.
5. Ask students to answer the questions.

This can be done in several ways: as a team game with a time limit, as a discussion activity or students can be asked to research the answers in the Internet.

POLITENESS

Do you know where you should and should not do these things?

Unwrap flowers before you give them as a present.
Show the soles of your feet to someone when you are talking to them.
Put your hand in front of your mouth when you laugh.
Make a V sign (meaning victory) with your palm facing inwards.
Keep your hand on the table when you are eating.
Go through a door first (women).
Go through a door first (men).
Drop a cigarette in the street.
Pat small children on the head.
Give a clock as a present.

Remember
Although it is easy to get information of this kind, you should always approach it with caution as the rules may not apply in all situations. It is always best to ask people who are familiar with rules of etiquette and behaviour in the country concerned.

 How important do you think it is to have this information and to do these things correctly when you are a visitor to a country?

What advice of this type would you give someone visiting Great Britain or your country?

QUOTATIONS

Focus: definitions of culture

Duration: 20 minutes

Activity type:

Trainer's notes

1. Photocopy the task for each student.
2. Lead-in: Ask students (individually or in groups) to think about how they would define culture. Elicit a few responses before distributing the quotations.
3. Photocopy one copy of the quotations.
4. Cut the quotations up separately so each student has one (in a large group give two students one quotation).

Follow-up

- Ask students to find more definitions of culture or quotations they like about culture.
- Students write a summary of the responses they get.
- Students find more quotations on the Internet.
- Students think up their own quotations.

QUOTATIONS

Talk to as many people as possible about your quotation and then summarise their responses in the form of a short presentation.

"Those who know nothing of foreign languages know nothing of their own." - *Johann Wolfgang von Goethe*

"Cultural heritage define the uniqueness of individuals. Appreciate cultural diversity." - *Lailah Gifty Akita*

"How you look at it is pretty much how you'll see it."
- *Rasheed Ogunlaru*

"What would it be like to have not only color vision but culture vision, the ability to see the multiple worlds of others." - *Mary Catherine Bateson*

"Culture is a little like dropping an Alka-Seltzer into a glass – you don't see it, but somehow it does something." - *Hans Magnus Enzensberger*

"Three criteria inspire as well as cultivate intercultural trust - sincerity, competence and reliability."
- *Sherwood Fleming*

"Culture hides more than it reveals, and strangely enough what it hides, it hides most effectively from its own participants." - *Edward T. Hall*

*for more QUOTATIONS go to page 65

RESPONSES

Focus: polite discourse

Duration: 10 minutes

Activity type:

Trainer's notes

1. Photocopy the task for each student.
2. Lead-in: Ask students how the word *No* is used in their language.
3. Students work individually and then compare answers.

Follow-up

Ask students to think of more situations where they have to avoid using the word *No*.

RESPONSES

How can you answer the following without using the word NO? Think of situations where you would have to answer the question with *no* and then think of as many ways of doing this as possible.

1. Would you like a glass of milk?
2. Would you like to go to the cinema this evening?
3. Do you like my dress?
4. Was my presentation good?
5. Could you help me with this?
6. Do you know where the railway station is?
7. Can you translate this into English?
8. Do you like Chinese food?
9. Have you ever visited my country?
10. Would you like to visit my country?

STRANGE AND NORMAL

Focus: cultural assumptions

Duration: 20 minutes

Activity type:

Trainer's notes

1. Photocopy the task sheet.
2. Lead-in: Write one pair of words on the board (e.g. disgusting / delicious) and ask students to think of one thing which could be described with both these words.
3. Explain to students that they are going to discuss more things like this, i.e. different views of the same thing. Ask them if they can think of any more examples.
4. Hand out the task sheet and let them discuss the first stage in pairs or groups before going on to the second stage. If necessary, fold the sheet along the line before handing it out.
5. Groups report back on their discussions.

Follow-up

Ask students to think of more examples from their own cultures which might be seen differently by others. Discuss these with the whole group.

STRANGE AND NORMAL

Look at these pairs of words. What do they have in common? Can you imagine that two people could use them to describe the same thing? Discuss this with a partner.

clean – dirty
cruel – entertaining
disgusting – delicious
funny – embarrassing
honest – showing off

modest – self-effacing
normal – strange
polite – rude
sharing – cheating
speaking – whispering

Now decide how you would describe these things and discuss this with your partner. What does this tell you about the way things are seen in different cultures?

1. A bull-fight
2. A Christmas tree
3. A reaction to a compliment
4. A restaurant
5. Accepting something the first time it is offered
6. Blowing your nose into a handkerchief
7. Food
8. Giving information in a low voice
9. Talking about what you can do well
10. Telling someone the answers to a test in class

TIME

Focus: cultural assumptions

Duration: 30 minutes

Activity type:

Trainer's notes

1. Photocopy the task sheet.
2. Lead-in: Ask students how punctual they are and whether they think it is necessary to always be on time. When do they come before an agreed time and when later? What do they understand when they are asked to be somewhere "in the morning", "immediately" "at 8 o'clock"?
3. Explain to students that they are going to read and discuss a critical incident.
4. Hand out the task sheet and let them read the incident. Clarify any language problems.
5. Discuss the questions about the incident and ask them to think of as many ideas as possible.
6. Discuss the second set of questions.

Follow-up

Students imagine Ramón has written to them to ask what happened. They write a reply to Ramón based on the discussion in the group.

TIME

Can you explain what is going on here? What are the reasons for the misunderstanding? How can knowledge of cultural differences help you to avoid conflicts like this? What can you do to resolve the conflict if it happens?

Not turning up for a meeting

Ramón, a Spanish student of Business Administration at the University of Santander, had applied for an internship at a German company in Frankfurt. During the exchange of emails they had, the HR manager had expressed interest in offering him a 3-month internship. Ramón's German was fairly good and he had some skills and qualifications which were of interest to the company. As Ramón knew that he would be in Frankfurt for a week a few months beforehand, he suggested that he could come along to the company so that the HR manager could meet him personally. This suggestion was met with enthusiasm and Ramón was invited to an interview at 10 a.m. on a particular day. Unfortunately Ramón overslept slightly and had not realised how long it would take him to get to the company from the friend's house where he was staying, so he only arrived at the company at 10:55. He was told that the HR manager was no longer available to see him so went into town and did some shopping. He was surprised when he received an email shortly afterwards saying that the internship would no longer be available for him.

HOT QUESTIONS

1. *What happened?*
2. *What are the reasons for the reactions of the HR manager?*
3. *What was Ramón's mistake?*
4. *What should he have done?*
5. *What can he do and say now?*

1. How would you define punctuality?
2. What is your attitude to being on time?
3. Have you ever been late for an appointment?
4. How do you decide on and fix an appointment?
5. What can happen if you arrive late for an appointment?
6. How do you feel about unpunctuality?

UNIVERSALS

Focus: cultural universals

Duration: 15 minutes

Activity type:

Trainer's notes

1. Photocopy the task for each student.
2. Students work individually or in small groups.
3. Discuss their opinions.

Follow-up

Ask students if they can think of any more examples.

UNIVERSALS

Choose 3 or 4 of the terms and decide first how you understand them / what they mean to you / how they are understood in your culture.

LAW
LOVE
PETS
MUSIC
SPORTS
HOLIDAYS
MARRIAGE
EDUCATION
FRIENDSHIP
PARENTAL DUTY

Discuss your understanding with the other students. What differences do you find?

VERY BAD BEHAVIOUR

Focus: cultural assumptions

Duration: 20 minutes

Activity type:

Trainer's notes

1. Photocopy the task sheet.
2. Lead-in: Write the word *cheating* on the board and ask students to define what they mean by it / what it means in their culture. How is it punished?
3. Explain to students that they are going to read and discuss a critical incident.
4. Hand out the task sheet and let them read the incident. Clarify any language problems.
5. Discuss the questions about the incident and ask them to think of as many ideas as possible.
6. Discuss the second set of questions.

Follow-up

Students imagine Lukas has written to them to ask what happened. They write a reply to Lukas based on the discussion in the group and give him some advice.

VERY BAD BEHAVIOUR

Can you explain what is going on here? What are the reasons for the misunderstanding? Can knowledge of cultural differences help you to avoid conflicts like this and how?

Cheating

Lukas was a German university student spending a semester at a university in California, USA. Before a class quiz, he prepared a piece of paper to take into the quiz and help him answer the questions. He showed this to one of his US fellow-students, Jim, before the quiz. Jim seemed shocked. After that no-one was very friendly to Lukas and he had rather a difficult time.

HOT QUESTIONS

1. How would you define cheating?
2. What is your attitude to cheating?
3. Have you ever cheated?
4. Is it a problem to discuss cheating with other students?
5. Do teachers know it goes on?
6. Should it be punished?
7. How?

1. *What happened?*
2. *What are the reasons for the reactions of the other students?*
3. *What was Lukas' mistake?*
4. *What should he have done?*
5. *What can he do and say now?*

WHERE WOULD(N'T) YOU?

Focus: polite behaviour

Duration: 20 minutes

Activity type:

Trainer's notes

1. Photocopy the task for each student.
2. Students answer the questions individually and then discuss their answers with others.

KEY - WHERE WOULD(N'T) YOU?

Where would you…	Where wouldn't you …
1. USA	6. South Korea Italy
2. The Netherlands Sweden	7. India Arabic countries
3. Russia Italy	8. India Asian Arabic countries
4. Spain South America	9. India
5. USA	10. Arabic countries

WHERE WOULD (N'T) YOU?

Do you know the answers to these questions?
Compare your answers with other students.

Where would you...

1. ... wait for a waiter to show you to a table in a restaurant?
2. ... take off your shoes before going into someone's house?
3. ... always take a receipt when you pay for something?
4. ... kiss someone at the first meeting?
5. ... help yourself to a drink from the fridge in someone else's home?

Where wouldn't you...

1. ... give a tip to a waiter?
2. ... admire things in someone's house so your host doesn't give them to you?
3. ... use your left hand to eat?
4. ... shake a woman's hand?
5. ... ask to meet someone's wife?

X-WORD

Focus: intercultural theory

Duration: 20 minutes

Activity type:

Trainer's notes

1. Photocopy the task sheet.
2. Hand out the task sheet.
3. Students complete the sentences.
4. Check the answers.

Follow-up

Students make up their own sentences with missing terms from intercultural theory and test each other.

KEY - X-WORD

1. low
2. conventions
3. contract
4. intercultural
5. meta
6. corporate
7. dimensions
8. individualism
9. taboo
10. chronic

X-WORD

Complete the following expressions.

1. High and .... context were used by Edward T. Hall to describe cultures.
2. Politeness .... are accepted ways of behaving politely in a culture.
3. The term "conversational ...." is used to describe agreed ways of communicating in groups.
4. .... competence consists of knowledge, attitudes and communication.
5. ....-communication is communication about communication.
6. .... culture is the culture of a company.
7. Cultural .... were used by scholars like Hofstede and Trompenaars to describe cultural differences.
8. .... and collectivism were defined by Hofstede to describe one way in which cultures are different.
9. .... topics are topics which should not be mentioned.
10. Poly or mono......................... describes how cultures see time.

YOU THINK...

Focus: appropriate reactions

Duration: 20 minutes

Activity type:

Trainer's notes

1. Photocopy the task for each student.
2. Lead-in: Ask students (individually or in groups) for situations when it is difficult or impolite for them to say what they think (e.g. when they think a dish they are offered looks disgusting, when they can't remember someone's name).
3. Tell students the following:
   In a group of international students it is important to be polite and not always say what you think. This is particularly important when you do not know someone very well and want to maintain the relationship.
4. Cut the page into cards. If you want to use these again they can be copied onto card and laminated.
5. Give one set of cards to each group.
6. The cards can be used in various ways, depending on the group and the size. The aim is always to match them up.
- Place cards face down on a table and turn them over one by one (memory / Pelmanism).
- Give each student a card. They walk around and read out what is on the card to find their partner.
- Distribute half the cards, either the polite or impolite versions. With polite versions, students can decide on a situation when they would say this. With the impolite version, they decide on the polite version. They then get the other set and compare them with their own answers. This can also be done in two groups who then get together.

Follow-up

- Think of more difficult situations and what you think and say.
- Decide when you could use the direct / rude versions and with whom.

YOU THINK...

SET 1

You have tried some new food at a party and you are offered more. *This food tastes disgusting.*	You are in a seminar. *I feel really sick.*
At a party someone keeps talking to you. *I wish you would leave me alone.*	Someone starts smoking in a no-smoking area. *You mustn't smoke here.*
A fellow-student asks you why his grades are always low. *You should work harder.*	A fellow-student asks for your help with an essay. *I don't want to do that.*
You want a book which you can't reach. *Give me that book.*	A fellow-student asks you for feedback on a presentation. *Your presentation was awful.*
A fellow-student comes at 6 p.m. to an appointment you made for 5 p.m. *Why are you late?*	A fellow-student asks what you think of her dress. *I don't like your dress.*
You meet a fellow-student one morning. *You look terrible.*	At a party you are offered a drink. *I don't want a drink.*
You don't eat meat and are offered meat at a party. *I don't eat meat.*	A group of students want to go to the swimming pool. *I would hate to do that.*

*for SET TWO go to page 66

QUIZZZ

Focus: facts about Britain

Duration: 15 minutes

Activity type:

Trainer's notes

1. Photocopy the task sheet for each student.
2. Tell students to answer the questions individually and then compare their answers with a partner.
3. Those who finish quickly can then think of more questions about Britain.

Follow-up

Students write a quiz like this about their country or another country.

KEY - QUIZZZ

1. England, Wales, Scotland, Northern Ireland. The capitals are London, Cardiff, Edinburgh and Belfast.
2. Queen Elizabeth II
3. Prince Charles, Prince William, Prince George
4. 1966
5. Ben Nevis (Scotland)
6. The river Thames
7. Saint George
8. Union Jack
9. 2012
10. Paul McCartney, John Lennon, George Harrison, Ringo Starr, Liverpool

QUIZZZ

Here are some questions to see how much you know about Britain. Write down your answers and check them with a partner.

1. How many countries belong to the United Kingdom and what are their capitals?
   _____
   _____

2. What is the name of the Queen?
   _____

3. Who are the next three people in line for the throne?
   _____

4. When did England win the World Cup?
   _____

5. What is the highest mountain in the United Kingdom?
   _____

6. Which river runs through London?
   _____

7. Who is the patron saint of England?
   _____

8. What is another name for the British flag?
   _____

9. When were the Olympic Games last held in Britain?
   _____

10. Can you name all four Beatles and say which city they are from?
    _____
    _____

CRITICAL INCIDENTS

Task sheet B

A critical incident
- happens unexpectedly
- produces negative reactions or feelings
- makes an impression
- needs a solution

Tell your partner what happens in this incident, ask and answer questions and discuss possible solutions. Listen to your partner's incident and do the same. Then discuss the differences.

 **Confidential! Do not show this text to your partner!**

> Song Xu from China was in Germany to improve his German and was asked to teach some Chinese conversation classes at a local university. In the first lesson he introduced himself as "Teacher" in Chinese and was surprised when the students gave him their first names and told him their age and hobbies. Then he asked them to copy down Chinese characters and to repeat some words all together. Their Chinese was quite advanced and Song Xu praised them but they did not seem very happy and some left the class. Some students looked at their Smartphones and some left the room and came back in a few minutes later. They smiled a lot and talked to each other. At the end of the class they all knocked on the table.

E-MAILS

Your email address:
Use an email address which is also suitable for formal situations.

Length:
Keep your email short but don't forget the most important things!

Subject line:
This should tell the recipient what is in the message.

Salutation:
This must be appropriate. It is best to write Dear … if you are not sure. Hello / Hi are informal and only for friends or people you know well.

Title:
Use the correct title. Miss is usually only used for little girls. Use Ms for a woman and Mr for a man. Professor and Dr are not used with Mr or Ms.

Close:
Best regards or Best wishes are acceptable in most situations.

Main message:
Make sure this is clear and appropriate.

Politeness:
Do not just state your main message. Start with the reason for your email, especially if you are requesting something or apologising for a mistake. End with an appropriate polite acknowledgement or thanks. Use the "sandwich" method – polite beginning – main message – polite end.

Spelling:
Use a spell checker and read your email through carefully before you send it.

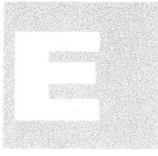

FOOD

Are there things which people in your country eat which others may find unpleasant or difficult to eat? Think also of combinations or ways of cooking and not only ingredients.

Is there any British food which you find difficult to eat?

Which of these ways of refusing food do you find acceptable / polite?

Remember
Food is often a very sensitive topic, so it is important to be careful about how you refuse food in different cultures.

It's delicious, but I'm afraid I can't eat anything at the moment.

I'm sorry I'm not allowed to eat that.

I don't find … very appetising.

In my country we think that … is inedible.

Eating … is rather unusual for me.

I don't normally eat ….

QUOTATIONS

Talk to as many people as possible about your quotation and then summarise their responses in the form of a short presentation.

"No culture can live if it attempts to be exclusive."
- *Mahatma Gandhi*

"Every man's ability may be strengthened or increased by culture." - *John Abbott*

"Culture is the collective programming of the mind."
- *Geert Hofstede*

"If we are going to live with our deepest differences then we must learn about one another." - *Deborah J. Levine*

"To become a true global citizen, one must abandon all notions of 'otherness' and instead embrace 'togetherness'."
- *Suzy Kassem*

"Language is the road map of a culture. It tells you where its people come from and where they are going."
- *Rita Mae Brown*

"The crucial differences which distinguish human societies and human beings are not biological. They are cultural."
- *Ruth Benedict*

YOU THINK...

SET 2

I'm afraid I can't eat any more.	*I don't feel very well.*
I've just seen someone I know and must go and talk to them.	*Smoking is not allowed in public buildings.*
Maybe you should concentrate a little more on your work.	*I'm afraid I haven't got time to do that today.*
Could you give me that book, please?	*There were one or two things in your presentation you could improve.*
Didn't we arrange to meet at 5 p.m.?	*I really like the blue dress you wore yesterday.*
Are you feeling okay? You don't look very well.	*No, thank you, I'm not thirsty.*
No thank you, I'm a vegetarian.	*Could we do something else instead?*

A-Z Activity Series

A–Z Activities is the new series of photocopiable resource books from Academic Study Kit.

Each book contains a collection of activities for communication practice. The material is organised in a photocopiable format with user-friendly trainer's notes, outlining the language focus, type of activity and timing. Suitable for intermediate to advanced learners.

FEATURES

- pairwork and groupwork tasks
- problem-solving discussions
- meetings and mini presentations
- vocabulary games
- deduction activities
- dictoglosses

OTHER TITLES IN THE SERIES

A-Z of Business Activities
Julie Pratten

A-Z of Global Issues
Julie Pratten, Linda Ruas and Helen Waldron

A-Z of Coaching
Ben Dobbs and Michelle Hunter

A-Z of ESOL
Emily Bryson

All titles are available in print and digital format.

www.academicstudykit.com

Teach outside the box!

www.ingramcontent.com/pod-product-compliance
Lightning Source LLC
Chambersburg PA
CBHW081356230426
43667CB00017B/2847